MR.
WRONG

A USER'S GUIDE

BY THE SAME AUTHORS

••••

101 Uses for a Bridesmaid Dress

CINDY WALKER

ILLUSTRATIONS BY

DONNA MEHALKO

WILLIAM MORROW

AN IMPRINT OF HARPER COLLINS PUBLISHERS

How to Use a Guy How to Use a Guy How to Use a Guy

MR.
WRONG

A USER'S GUIDE

It is the policy of William Morrow and Company, Inc., and its imprints and affiliates, recognizing the importance of preserving what has been written, to print the books we publish on acid-free paper, and we exert our best efforts to that end.

Library of Congress Cataloging-in-Publication Data has been applied for.

ISBN 0-688-17025-0

Printed in Mexico

First Edition

1 2 3 4 5 6 7 8 9 10

Book design by Chris Welch

www.williammorrow.com

To all the men who made this book possible

We're all familiar with the old proverb "A bird in the hand is worth two in the bush." I think it has something to do with learning to appreciate what you have instead of mooning over what you don't. Especially when it comes to guys . . .

So what is a girl to do in between Mr. Rights? I say, go out, enjoy life, experiment, see the world! The men you meet along the way should not be considered a waste of time. If that bird in your hand is not The One, don't just set him free. Make use of him.

Does this sound familiar?

A. You meet him at a bar, and at a glance you know that he's not your type, but you're in between boyfriends, so why the heck not?

B. He's the NGB (a nice guy, but . . .) your best friend has set you up with. You prefer the withdrawn, silent type, but you'll try anything once.

C. You have the Whitman's Sampler theory of dating. (You prefer the nuts and chews, but if those are already taken, you'll settle for the cream centers, at least for one bite.)

D. Your mother warned you never to marry an unemployed musician. You know that she's right. But you're young still, so why not have some fun before you settle down and move to the suburbs.

E. He's not the man of your dreams, but he's Mr. Right Now.

If so, I've got some ideas for you . . .

MR.
WRONG

A USER'S GUIDE

Sweetly ask him to be your cat-sitter (when a better Mr. Wrong asks you to go on a winter vacation to St. Bart's).

• • • •

A devoted, self-employed type who has flexible hours can also be a chauffeur. Taxis are *so* expensive.

A tennis instructor can teach you some new moves. After all, you wouldn't want the future father of your children to know that you have no hand/eye coordination. It doesn't hurt if your tennis instructor looks like Robert Redford either. Ball? What ball?

• • • •

Use him to make your ex jealous or catch the eye of the man you're really pursuing. Just like it's easier to get a job if you have one, it's easier to get a man if you have one.

Date an auto mechanic and drive his vintage foreign sports car while he's fixing yours.

Date a pilot and fly free all over the world. First class, of course.

M r. Wrong can be a sex instructor. (You want to be the Total Woman to your future husband, and you've gotta learn somewhere.)

Ever thought of becoming a blonde, or shaving your head à la Sinéad O'Connor? You can try out new looks on a live Mr. Wrong without running the risk of scaring off your future husband.

The Gardener. Find a guy who loves to trim hedges. It gives him pride and saves you money.

• • • •

Also, why buy a bookshelf when you can have Mr. Fix-It make it for you?

Date an Amish man, so you can really get away from it all on the weekends.

• • • •

Find relief from parental pressures by introducing an obvious Mr. Wrong to the family. Suddenly, no one will be asking about wedding plans.

If you always wished you were to the manner born, marry impoverished royalty. After the divorce, you get to keep your title.

● ● ● ●

For those cool, calculating women who always go after power, the right Mr. Wrong can provide career advancement.

Rebel and scandalize your uptight WASP relatives by running off with a biker.

He may not be the sharpest knife in the drawer, but a well-muscled guy can always be your bodyguard. Pretend you're someone famous, and get the best table at the hottest restaurant.

In the cruel (but we caught you laughing) category, even the most useless man is good for something—you just have to figure out what that is:

Surfboard

Ottoman

Sunblock

Ashtray

Coatrack

Date a psychiatrist. I think that's called transference, but by any name, it saves on those enormous hourly fees they charge. And maybe he can cure you of the terrible habit you have of dating the wrong men.

• • • •

Date an IRS agent and wreak vengeance on all your enemies. There is nothing like an audit to ruin one's day.

Learn a new language—date a foreigner (what they call the "immersion" technique).

Travel guide—let Mr. Wrong show you the world.

How about a mover? If your lease runs out, or you get kicked out of your illegal sublet, you'll need someone to move all your precious things to your next apartment.

Floor refinisher—to work on your next apartment so that the floors are beautiful by the time you move in.

● ● ● ●

Antique restorer—to refinish all those old pieces of furniture you buy at the flea market. Those paint-stripping chemicals are murder on your hands!

Rule a country; date a dictator.

● ● ● ●

Date a tax attorney, so you can defend yourself against a rival who's dating an IRS agent.

Y ou love your dog, but if Mr. Wrong wants to walk him…

A platonic Mr. Wrong can be your roommate—rent is sky-high.

• • • •

Housekeeper. Date a neat freak, and you'll never see a dust bunny again.

A florist will send you flowers every day. Everyone in the office will turn green with jealousy.

• • • •

Date a cashmere-goat farmer. His spinster sister can knit you six-ply sweaters and blankets.

Date a golf instructor—he knows how to drive a hole in one.

Date a professional rider and saddle him up.

Masseur. A man who's good with his hands is nothing to sneeze at.

• • • •

Footloose and fancy-free. Date a podiatrist. A little injection here, a tiny snip there, and you can still make the club that night in your Prada pumps.

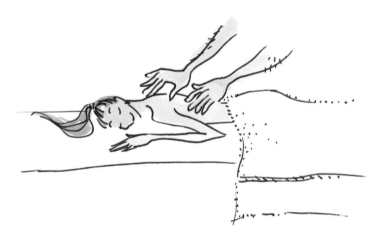

If you've always wanted to star in a music video, or have a song written about you, get cozy with a rock star.

● ● ● ●

Date a video clerk—never rewind again.

Try an electrician on for size.
Not only can he put up that
adorable crystal chandelier you
found at the flea market, he can
also get you free cable. I want my
MTV!

There's nothing better than dating a dentist, especially if he does cosmetic work. Change your fillings from silver to white, fix that nasty chip, bleach all your pearly whites, and get a little laughing gas while you're at it.

If you need a new look, let him take you shopping.

• • • •

Dinner—a girl's gotta eat.

• • • •

Rent—a girl's gotta have a roof over her head.

Flirt, flirt, flirt. It's an art form you want to perfect for the day you *do* meet Mr. Right. Especially if you're out of practice. So if you've just come back from an extended trip to Uzbekistan, have been spending 24-7 with your new baby niece, or have just signed walking papers and find yourself "out there" again, give that man at the bar a coy look. Go ahead!

• • • •

The spice of life. Even the worst Mr. Wrong can provide variety. And sometimes a bad man can be very good indeed.

If you're a single mother, let Mr. Wrong play baby-sitter while you go out and find your children a daddy.

● ● ● ●

Mr. Wrong can be The Wallet. Stock up on nice things because you and Mr. Right will have to save for college tuition.

A trainer can help you get into shape. Gym memberships are so expensive!

• • • •

If you hook up with a sports agent, you can go to all the best sporting events, sit in the best seats, and run off with Derek Jeter.

Date a magician—he can make your hips disappear.

A hypnotist can cure you of such evil habits as cigarette smoking, Hershey's chocolate eating, diet Coke drinking, and emotionally unavailable men dating.

Date a painter—become the new *Mona Lisa*.

• • • •

How about a plastic surgeon? They always see a woman as a work-in-progress. Let him make you a work of art.

The right sort of Mr. Wrong can provide you with fifteen minutes of fame; a high-profile affair can make you more famous than eight years of graduate school and discovering the location of Noah's ark.

● ● ● ●

Date a lawyer because you never know when you'll need one.

Get cozy with an FBI agent and find out the real truth about UFOs.

Date a physicist and discover what they really mean when they talk about the Big Bang.

Can't drive a stick shift? Date a driving instructor and you'll be switching gears with ease.

Earn a Ph.D. in your spare time—date your professor.

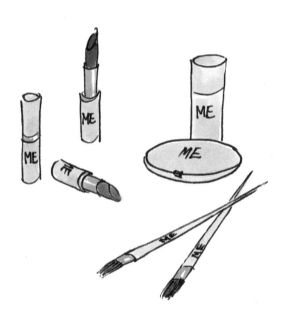

Date a biochemist and have him help you start your own cosmetics company.

● ● ● ●

Then find a computer nerd to create a website for your new Internet company. You could become a millionaire overnight!

He's the ideal New Year's Eve date.

● ● ● ●

Date a mortician—have your Halloween party at his "office."

Not every plumber displays butt crack and sports a beer gut. Call him when you've got *any* plumbing problems.

• • • •

Have all your furniture recovered by your new upholsterer boyfriend. It would be embarrassing to entertain Mr. Right on your shabby plaid hand-me-down couch.

Wow your future husband by learning basic cooking skills and knowing the difference between chervil and fennel—date a chef!

● ● ● ●

Win over potential friends and lovers! Be nice to Mr. Wrong, and he will spread the word of how wonderful you are.

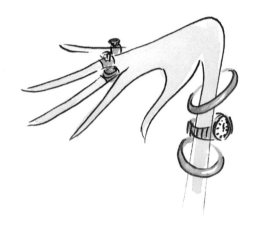

Date a jeweler because diamonds are a girl's best friend but a Rolex is pretty nice, too. So is a Cartier bracelet, classic diamond earrings, a triple-strand pearl choker…

Drive a brand-new car every year—date a car dealer.

Take the poor guy on vacation—he can carry your bags.

• • • •

Bring Mr. Wrong to holiday dinners like Thanksgiving and Christmas to distract you from your crazy family members.

Have you exhausted your own network of available men? Anyone can be your foot in the door. Once you have infiltrated his circle of friends, trade up.

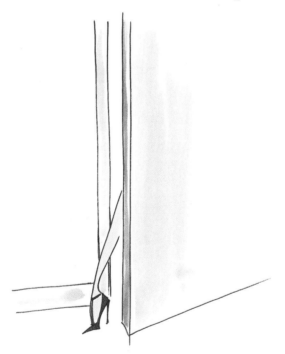

Date a media mogul and have him set you up with your very own talk show: *The Me Show*.

Date a yoga instructor.
Darling, it's amazing the
positions this man can get you
into. Let him help you reach
nirvana.

• • • •

Haven't you always wanted to
make love in front of the
penguin tank? You can, if you
date a zookeeper.

Firemen have those big hoses. You know, to put out fires with?

• • • •

Arm candy. If you get invited to an important function, it's sometimes nice to bring an eye-catching date.

They say that chocolates are a girl's (second) best friend. Go out with a candy man and discover why.

Fondue is a ballet term, you know. Date a ballet dancer and learn how to do the splits.

A hairdresser is sure to give you a free blowout whenever you want.

• • • •

Date a decorator. He may not ravish you in bed, so let him fluff your living room. It's amazing how just the right touches can warm up a space!

Spider and cockroach killer.

• • • •

Afraid of the dark? A guy is a good bogeyman repellant.

Date a Latin man—learn to tango.

● ● ● ●

Afterward, you might consider a brief encounter with a chiropractor.

Date an astronaut and see if zero gravity prevents sagging.

Better yet, find yourself a mad scientist who can build you a time machine. Didn't we all look our best when we were eighteen?

Learn self-defense—date a cop. Other perks: Speeding and parking tickets will become a thing of the past because he tells his friends and colleagues to leave you alone.

• • • •

Date a banker—avoid paying ATM fees.

Are you the next Michelangelo? Mr. Wrong can be your model—for free!

● ● ● ●

If *you're* a model, date your agent, so he'll promote you more enthusiastically.

Date a clergyman—start building equity for your Afterlife.

Or a comedian—at least you'll have some laughs.

Date a trapeze artist and swing from the chandelier.

• • • •

Or a lion tamer, if you're partial to whips and glitter. Also, if he can deal with such a dangerous animal, he will certainly know how to get along with your overprotective father.

Find immortality—break an author's heart and he will write a book about you. Then again, you might get a book idea of your own if you date enough Mr. Wrongs!